Easy-to-Make
WATER TOYS
That Really Work

Mary Blocksma
&
Dewey Blocksma

illustrated by Art Seiden

Prentice-Hall, Inc.
Englewood Cliffs, New Jersey

To our Dad,
Ralph Blocksma,
who taught us to love the water

Printed in the United States of America •J

Prentice-Hall International, Inc., London
Prentice-Hall of Australia, Pty. Ltd., Sydney
Prentice-Hall Canada, Inc., Toronto
Prentice-Hall of India Private Ltd., New Delhi
Prentice-Hall of Japan, Inc., Tokyo
Prentice-Hall of Southeast Asia Pte. Ltd., Singapore
Whitehall Books Limited, Wellington, New Zealand
Editora Prentice-Hall do Brasil LTDA., Rio de Janeiro
Prentice-Hall Hispanoamericana, S.A., Mexico

10 9 8 7 6 5 4 3 2

Book Design by Constance Ftera

Library of Congress Cataloging in Publication Data

Blocksma, Mary.
    Easy-to-make water toys that really work.

    Summary: Instructions for making toys that move
in water.
    1. Toys—Juvenile literature.   2. Toy making—
Juvenile literature.   [1. Toy making.   2. Handicraft]
I. Blocksma, Dewey.   II. Title.   III. Title: Water
toys that really work.
TT174.B56 1984   745.592   84-24913
ISBN 0-13-223561-7

ACKNOWLEDGEMENTS

Our grateful thanks to Dylan Kuhn from Laramie, Wyoming,
and to Michelle Triolo from San Jose, California,
for helping with toys for this book
when they were twelve

CONTENTS

MAKE A GREAT TOY BETTER!

Look what a kid like you can do with a stack of styrofoam, a pack of balloons, and a plastic straw or two! Poke a hole, cut and tape, and in minutes you will have one of the water toys in this book.

You will find step-by-step directions for 29 toys. Use the easy suggestions in the many Experiment paragraphs to make more toys. And when you think you've got the hang of it, turn to the chapter at the end of the book to get started making even more toys on your own.

But remember—making your toys is only half the fun. The other half is playing with them. All you need is water, and there are plenty of places to find that. Take your water toys to a nearby ocean or stream, or to one of our country's one-and-a-half million lakes, ponds, and reservoirs. Use a backyard or plastic pool. Or start the water in the most popular waterhole of all, the bathtub.

Wherever you find it, water is the biggest, cheapest, handiest toy in the world. But you can make it even better. All you need are two simple tools and a few supplies.

WHAT YOU NEED

Tools and Supplies

A pair of *scissors* and a *pencil* are the only tools you will need to make any toy in this book. You can buy most of the materials from your neighborhood supermarket.

1 package of styrofoam plates: Big dinner plates work best, but the lunch size will do fine.

1 package of styrofoam cups: Get the medium, coffee-cup size.

Long and round balloons: Buy medium-sized or big balloons. The kind used with helium work well. Good-quality balloons are stronger and last longer.

1 package of plastic straws: Get the kind with "elbows" that bend.

Plastic tape: You can buy waterproof plastic tape in many bright colors. You can also use black electrician's tape or silver duct tape. DO NOT USE CELLOPHANE TAPE OR MASKING TAPE: they won't stick after they get wet.

Rubber cement: When you need to glue a water toy, *always* use rubber cement.

Here are some other useful items:

clear Con-Tact paper
small styrofoam balls
metallic Mylar
inexpensive sponges
ballpoint pen
crayons
acrylic paints

Quick Tips

Here are some hints for making water-worthy toys:

1. *Cut styrofoam from the outside in.* This way it won't bend or break. If you get stuck, stop and start again from another outside point.

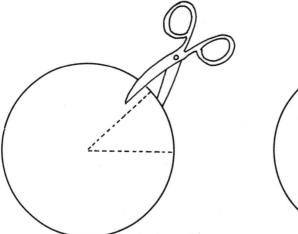 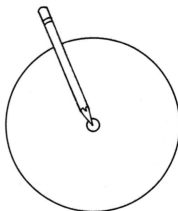

To cut a pie piece, make 2 cuts. Start each cut at the rim.

Poke holes with a pencil.

2. *Use a pencil to poke holes in styrofoam.* Pencil holes are nice and smooth, as well as just the right size to fit a plastic straw.

3. *Use waterproof tape.* Cellophane tape comes loose when it gets wet. Plastic tape will make your toys last a surprisingly long time.

4. *Use rubber cement to join pieces and make the joints waterproof.* Use plenty, and let it dry well before you get it wet.

5. *Draw your patterns lightly.* If you press too hard, your pen or pencil might go right through the styrofoam.

6. *When you work with Con-Tact paper, use small pieces.* It's harder to get the air bubbles out of large pieces.

7. *When you need to knot a balloon, you can often use this trick:*

Nifty Balloon Tie

WHAT YOU NEED

1 small piece of plastic straw   tape

WHAT YOU DO

1. Blow up the balloon. Hold the air in while you roll the lip over the piece of straw.

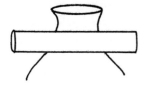

Step 1

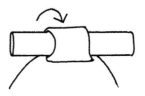

2. Bend the straw ends back until they meet.

3. Tape the ends together.

Step 2

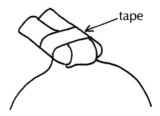

Step 3

Bright Ideas

Almost all styrofoam is white. Here are some waterproof ways to brighten it up.

1. *Use a ballpoint pen to draw lines on styrofoam.* Any color ink works well for drawing eyes, noses, mouths, or neat designs. (Don't use pens with erasable ink, though.)

2. *Color larger areas with crayons.* Colors take on a strange glow when crayoned on styrofoam.

3. *Jazz up your models with acrylic paints.* Acrylic paints are expensive, but if you have them, use them. They are bright and waterproof and will make your toys look terrific. Waterproof markers also work well.

4. *Decorate with busted balloons.* Cut balloon rubber into flags and tails to tape to your boats and fish. Or cut out rings, circles, or squares to glue with rubber cement into crazy designs.

PLAY IT SAFE!

You always have more fun when you play it safe, so be sure to remember these basic rules of water safety.

1. *Never take anything breakable into the water.* Glass is especially dangerous, because you can't see the sharp pieces.

2. *Never take anything sharp or pointed into the water.* Metal and wood can cut or jab you or leave splinters in your fingers.

3. *Always swim with a buddy and only when a parent, teacher, or lifeguard is there to watch you.*

4. *Stay seated in the tub,* except to get in or get out.

5. *Don't give your toys to babies.* The toys in this book were designed for kids over five years old. They are not good to eat! Don't put anything but balloons or straws in your mouth.

6. *Never use rubber cement near a fire or open flame, and make sure the room you're working in is well ventilated.*

7. *Always clean up after yourself.* Pick up all your toys and materials at the beach. At home, try keeping your bathtub toys in a kitchen-sized plastic trash container.

LOONY BALLOON

Here's a weird beach ball with a wacky wobble! Use a good balloon and this toy will be surprisingly tough.

What You Need

1 good-quality round balloon (the kind used with helium)

What You Do

1. Run water into the balloon. Fill it to the top.

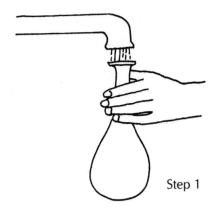

Step 1

2. Blow up the balloon.

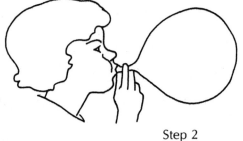

3. Knot the balloon, or use the Nifty Balloon Tie on page 9.

Step 2

Play With It! Throw your Loony Balloon, roll it, or just SMACK it on the water!

Experiment! Instead of a round balloon, use a long one. Be sure to force the air into the far end of the balloon when you blow it up.

BALLOON BOAT

Balloon boats catch the wind but won't tip over easily.

What You Need

1 styrofoam plate   pencil
1 round balloon

What You Do

1. Poke a hole in the center of the plate.

2. Poke the lip of the balloon through the hole. Blow up the balloon from the back of the plate.

3. Knot the balloon, or use the Nifty Balloon Tie on page 9.

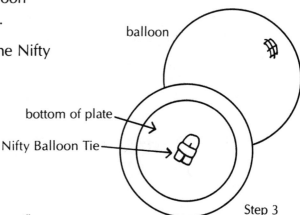

Step 2

balloon

bottom of plate

Nifty Balloon Tie

Step 3

Float It!   For an amazing party, float lots of bright Balloon Boats in a pool or lake! Race Balloon Boats by blowing on the balloons.

Experiment!   Use a big sponge or a fast-food carton instead of a plate.

WATER SPINNER

Turn a whirling top into a rocket or a burbling boat!

What You Need

1 round balloon   scissors
1 plastic straw   tape

What You Do

1. Cut the rolled lip off the balloon.

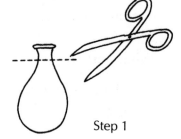

Step 1

2. Cut the straw in half. Poke one end of the bending half into the balloon.

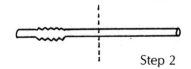

Step 2

3. Tape the balloon to the straw.

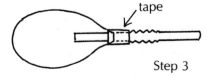

tape

Step 3

Make It Go! Blow up the balloon (if air leaks out, put on more tape). Pinch the straw and let it go in the air. For a boat, let it go under water. For a top, bend the straw and set the balloon on the water before letting go.

Experiment! To make the top spin faster, cut the straw off closer to the bend.

GO-BOAT

Use this simple balloon power on other boats as well.

What You Need

1 Water Spinner   pencil
  (page 14)
1 styrofoam plate

Step 1

What You Do

1. Make the Water Spinner on page
   14, *but don't cut the straw.*

Step 2

2. Poke a hole in the middle of the
   plate.

3. Pull the Water Spinner straw
   through the hole.

Make It Go!   Blow the balloon up through the straw. (If air leaks
out, put on more tape.) Pinch the end of the straw and put the
Go-Boat in the water. Make sure the straw is bent and is *under*
the water. Let go!

Experiment!   Instead of a plate,
use the Sun Boat (page 43), the
Balloon Pontoon (page 18),
or half of a fast-food carton.

MINI PUTT-PUTT

Here's a toy that makes wonderful noises. The bigger the balloon, the longer the Mini Putt-Putt putts.

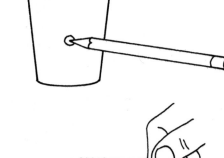

What You Need

1 Water Spinner   pencil
  (page 14)   tape
1 plastic straw
1 styrofoam cup

Step 1

What You Do

1. Poke a hole in the middle of the cup bottom. Poke another hole about ⅓ of the way up the side of the cup.

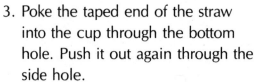

Step 2

2. Pinch the bending end of the straw flat. Tape the end shut, leaving only a tiny air hole.

leave a tiny air hole

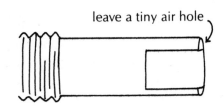

3. Poke the taped end of the straw into the cup through the bottom hole. Push it out again through the side hole.

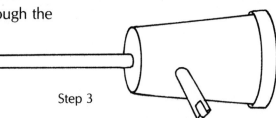

Step 3

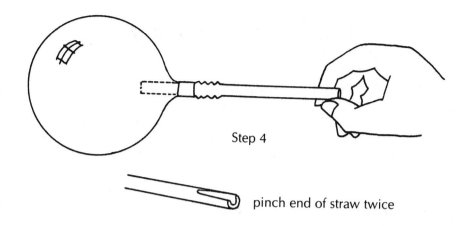

Step 4

pinch end of straw twice

4. Make the Water Spinner on page 14. Pinch the end of the straw flat. Fold it and pinch it again.

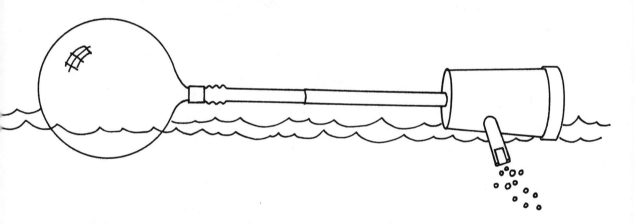

Make It Go!   Blow up the balloon through the straw. Pinch the end of the straw and stick it inside the cup straw. Set the Mini Putt-Putt in the water, making sure the "exhaust pipe" is under water.

Experiment!   Use a long balloon. Or instead of a cup, use a styrofoam plate with a hole in the middle.

BALLOON PONTOON

Use different colored balloons to give this pontoon boat extra pizzazz!

What You Need

2 long balloons   tape
1 styrofoam plate   scissors
4 plastic straws

What You Do

1. Tape the middles of two straws to the top edge of the plate. Tape the other two straws across from the first two (see drawing).

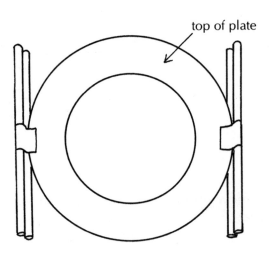

top of plate

Step 1

2. Blow up the balloons. Knot the ends, or use the Nifty Balloon Tie (page 9).

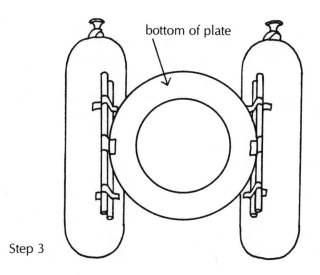

bottom of plate

Step 3

3. Turn the plate over. Tape the straws to the center of each balloon. (Make sure the balloons are straight *before* you tape!)

Float It!

Experiment!   To make a balloon raft without a plate, blow up two long balloons and set them side by side. Lay two straws across the balloons and tape one end of each straw to the first balloon and the other end to the second balloon. Turn the raft over and tape straws to the bottom of the raft the same way.

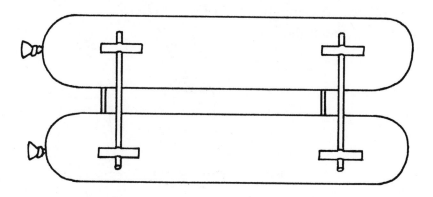

LOONY PONTOONY

One of the authors won a model-boat race on Lake Michigan with this wonderful boat!

What You Need

1 Balloon Pontoon   tape
   (page 18)   pencil
1 plastic straw   scissors
1 round balloon
1 styrofoam cup

What You Do

1. Make the Balloon Pontoon on page 18.

2. Blow up the round balloon and knot it.

3. Fold the bending end of the straw over the neck of the balloon. Tape.

4. Poke a hole in the middle of the cup bottom. Poke the free end of the straw through the hole.

tape

Step 3

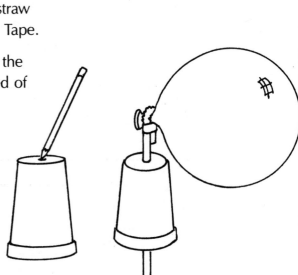

Step 4

5. Poke a hole in the middle of the Balloon Pontoon's plate. Poke the straw through the hole.

6. Turn the boat over. Pull on the straw until the cup is tight against the plate.

7. Cut two slits in the straw so it opens flat against the plate. Tape the tabs to the plate.

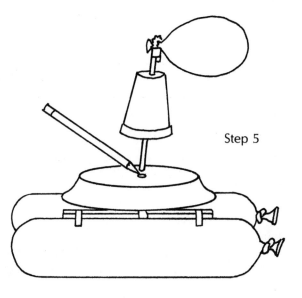

Step 5

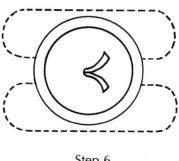

Step 6

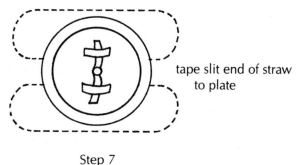

tape slit end of straw to plate

Step 7

Float It! To make it go faster, blow on the balloon.

Experiment! Cut out a styrofoam person to stick to the boat. (Tape the knees and elbows so they will bend without breaking.)

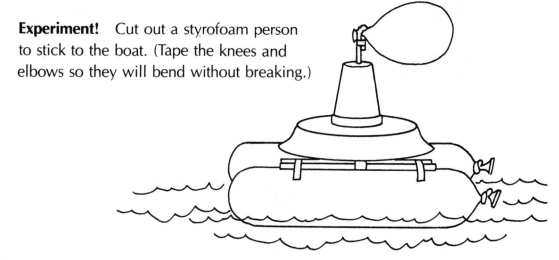

WATER WINGS

Here's a quick way to turn yourself into a butterfly. (Although they may hold you up, don't rely on these Water Wings for safety.)

What You Need

4 medium-sized or large balloons
4 pieces of cotton string (each about half the length of your arm)

What You Do

1. Blow up each balloon and knot it. (Don't use the Nifty Balloon Tie for this one.)

2. Tie one string to each balloon.

3. Gather two strings in each hand. Tie all four strings in a knot.

Step 3

Float on It!   Lie on your stomach across the knot. Let the balloons pop up behind your arms, like butterfly wings!

Experiment!   Try using different shapes of balloons.

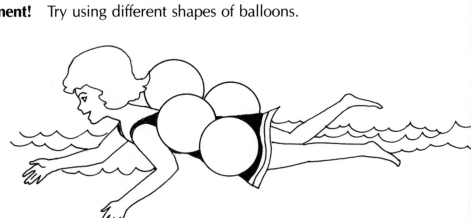

QUICK-TRICK RAFT

This quick-to-make raft is great fun, but never depend on balloons for safety.

What You Need

4 to 8 (or more) balloons, any shape or size
1 large plastic trash bag
scissors
tape

What You Do

1. Blow up each balloon and knot the end. (Don't use the Nifty Balloon Tie.)

2. Stuff the balloons into the trash bag.

Step 2

3. To close the bag, line up the open edges. Fold them over several times. Tape well.

tape end of bag closed

Step 3

Float on It! By pushing the balloons around, you can change the shape of your raft. (It doesn't matter if water gets inside the bag.)

Experiment! Use cotton string to tie your Quick-Trick Raft in one or more places to make different shapes.

RAFT CRAFT

Here's a flat raft that you can really float on—in shallow water, of course!

What You Need

4 to 8 long balloons (thin ones work best)
1 large plastic trash bag

scissors
lots of tape

What You Do

1. Lay the trash bag out flat. Cut three or four small, evenly-spaced holes through both layers of the bag along each lengthwise fold line.

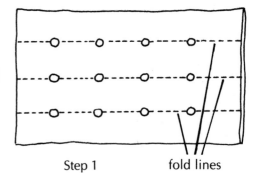

Step 1   fold lines

2. Put a piece of tape through one hole. Press tape to both sides of the bag.

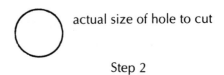

actual size of hole to cut

Step 2

3. Put another piece of tape on the other side of the hole.

4. Tape over the hole and the first two pieces of tape. Turn the bag over and tape over the same hole on that side.

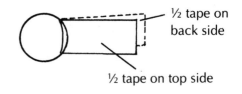

½ tape on back side

½ tape on top side

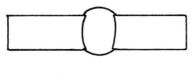

Step 3

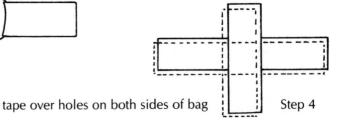

tape over holes on both sides of bag   Step 4

5. Follow Steps 2-4 to tape each hole in the bag.

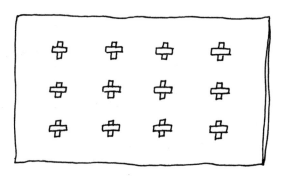

Step 5

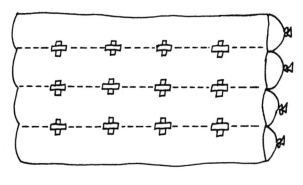

Step 6

6. Blow up the balloons and knot them (don't use the Nifty Balloon Tie.) Slide the balloons into the slots between the taped holes.

tape end of bag closed

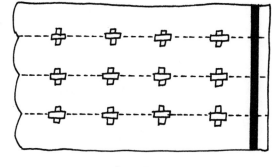

7. Fold the end of the bag shut. Tape it well.

Step 7

Float on It!   Use the Raft Craft as you would a toy air mattress.

Experiment!   Make a paddle board with a smaller plastic trash bag and fewer balloons.

WATER TILES

Water is the magic glue that holds these up for hours!

What You Need

clear plastic Con-Tact paper   scissors
brightly colored paper

What You Do

Step 1

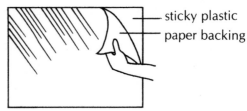

— sticky plastic
— paper backing

Step 2

1. Cut the colored paper into circles, squares, triangles, and rectangles the size of kids' blocks.

2. Cut a piece of Con-Tact paper about the size of this book. Lay it on the table, paper side up. Peel off the paper.

3. Set a few of the bright paper shapes on the sticky Con-Tact paper about this far ———— apart (about 1 inch).

Step 3

4. Cut and peel another piece of Con-Tact paper the same size as the first. Set it on top of the first piece, sticky side down.

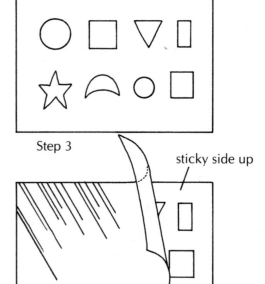

sticky side up

sticky side down

Step 4

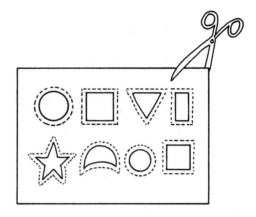

5. Smooth out any wrinkles or air bubbles. Then cut around each shape. Stay this far —— (about ½ inch) from the edges.

Step 5

6. Press around all the edges of each piece to make it waterproof.

7. Repeat Steps 2-6 until all the paper shapes are sandwiched in Con-Tact paper.

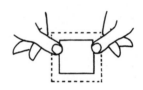

Step 6

Stick Them Up! Get the Water Tiles wet. Then stick them up on a tile or glass wall near the tub. Arrange the tiles to make faces or pictures.

Experiment! Make letters to spell out your name or special signs!

BUBBLE HOOP

Here come the monster bubble-balls!

What You Need

1 styrofoam plate   scissors

What You Do

Cut the middle out of the styrofoam plate. (Don't cut through the rim.)

cutting line

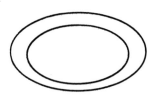

Blow Bubbles!   Nest the Bubble Hoop in a styrofoam plate holding bubble soap. Lift it out. Then wave the hoop in the air or blow through the middle.

Experiment!   Make a bubble castle: Instead of cutting out the middle of the plate, pour water in it until the plate is half full. Mix in 2 or 3 tablespoons of shampoo with your fingers. Use a straw to blow a big bubble on the top of the plate. Then blow bubbles around the big bubble, on top of it, or even inside it.

BIG BUB

This bubbler blows huge bubbles, and it's super-easy to make!

What You Need

1 styrofoam cup   pencil

What You Do

Poke a hole in the middle of the cup bottom.

Blow Bubbles!   Dip the open end of the cup in bubble soap and blow gently through the hole.

Experiment!   Make your own bubble soap: Pour 1 tablespoon of shampoo or dishwashing liquid, like Joy or Ivory, into a styrofoam plate. (DON'T use detergent for the washing machine or dishwasher.) Add 2 tablespoons of water. Mix with your finger. If it's too thick, add a little more water. And remember, never swallow ANY kind of bubble soap, homemade or the kind you buy.

BUBBLE BUILDER

Now you can make big globs of little bubbles.

What You Need

1 Big Bub (page 29)   scissors
some Con-Tact paper   pencil

What You Do

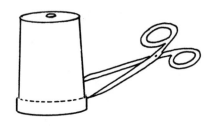

1. Make Big Bub (page 29). Then carefully cut the rim off the cup to make a ring. *Don't cut through the rim.*

Step 1

2. Set the ring on an unpeeled piece of Con-Tact paper. Trace around the ring.

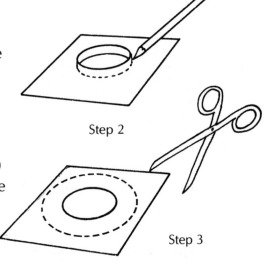

Step 2

3. Cut out the Con-Tact paper circle about this far ——— (¾ inch) from the traced circle. Peel off the paper. Set the plastic circle sticky side up on the table.

Step 3

4. Set Big Bub on the middle of the circle. Snip through the edge of the circle as far as the cup.

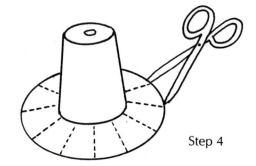

Step 4

5. Fold the tabs up against the cup.
   Slip the cup ring over the tabs.

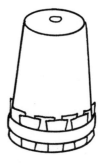

Step 5

6. Poke several holes in the Con-Tact
   circle.

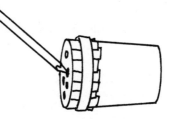

Step 6

Blow Bubbles!   Dip the plastic end of the Bubble Builder in your
bubble soap. Blow gently through the hole in the cup bottom.

Experiment!   Use a fast-food milkshake cup to make a bigger
Bubble Builder. Make bigger holes in the Con-Tact paper by
cutting them carefully with a sharp pointed scissors. Make the
biggest hole in the middle.

BUBBLE MACHINE

Make a mountain of bubbles with this nifty machine.

What You Need

1 styrofoam cup	scissors
1 styrofoam plate	pencil
1 plastic straw	tape
1 plate-size piece of	rubber cement
Con-Tact paper	

Step 1

What You Do

1. Poke a hole in the side of the cup near the bottom.

2. Poke the bending end of the straw into the hole. Tape well on the outside.

tape around hole

Step 2

3. Trace around the cup rim on the middle of the plate. Cut out the circle.

Step 3

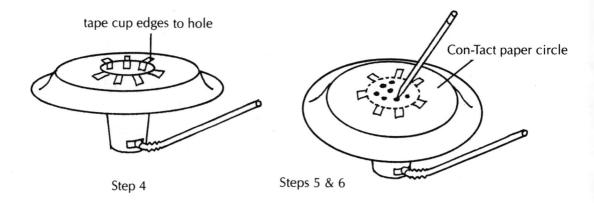

tape cup edges to hole

Con-Tact paper circle

Step 4　　　　　Steps 5 & 6

4. Set the plate upside down on the cup rim. Match the cup to the hole and tape.

5. Cut a circle of Con-Tact paper as big as the smooth inner part of the plate. Peel off the paper backing. Stick the circle to the plate, covering the cup hole.

6. Punch holes in the Con-Tact paper.

7. Paint the tape around the straw hole and the rim of the cup with lots of rubber cement. Let dry.

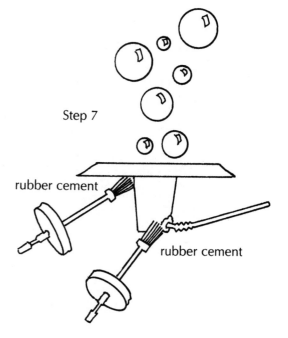

Step 7

rubber cement

rubber cement

Blow Bubbles!　Fill the cup halfway with water. Pour a few drops of shampoo through one of the holes. Blow through the straw until the bubbles look like a head of curly hair!

Experiment!　To make a floating bubble machine, use rubber cement to glue the cup bottom to another styrofoam plate. Let it dry before you use it.

SKEETER BOATS

These sailboats are so small,
you can float several in the sink.

What You Need

1 styrofoam plate   pencil
                        scissors

What You Do

1. Lightly draw two lines across the plate.

2. On one side of the plate, draw a boat shape between the two lines. Make a slot in the middle by pressing hard.

3. On the other side, draw a sail between the lines. Curve the mast under the line.

4. Carefully cut out the shapes. *(Remember to cut in from the outer edge.)* Fit the mast through the slot in the boat.

Float It!   Make a whole fleet of Skeeter Boats and race them!

Experiment!   Instead of a sail, draw a duck or a frog between the lines. Or make bigger toys by drawing the lines farther apart.

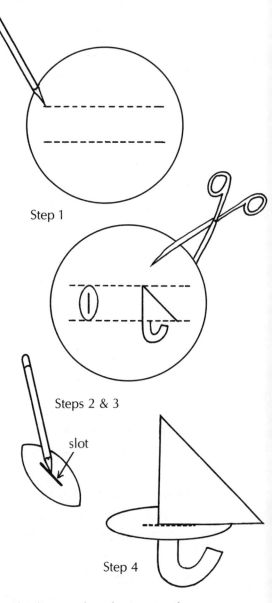

Step 1

Steps 2 & 3

slot

Step 4

MINI WHALE

Whales don't *have* to be enormous.

What You Need

1 styrofoam plate   scissors
                           ballpoint pen

What You Do

1. Draw a whale's body on the plate. Press hard to make slots for the fins and the tail.

2. Draw the tail and fins in the space that's left.

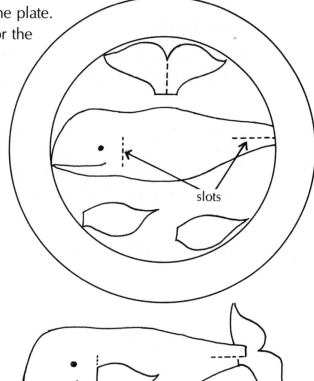

slots

3. Cut out the pieces and fit them together.

Float It!

Experiment! Make a swimmer by cutting out a person's body and putting legs and arms in slots!

SKATE BUG

This water bug slips and slides across the surface of a tub or pond.

What You Need

1 styrofoam plate

scissors
pencil
tape

What You Do

1. With a pencil, divide the plate into eight pie pieces. Cut out two of the pieces.

2. Draw two small diamond shapes on each cut-out piece (see drawing). Cut out the diamonds. Cut the pie-points off each piece.

3. Overlap the inner edges of the two pieces and tape them together.

Step 1

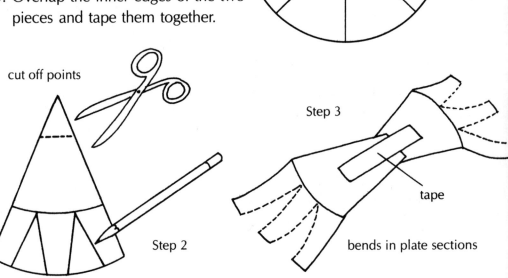

cut off points

Step 2

cut out diamond shapes

Step 3

tape

bends in plate sections

36

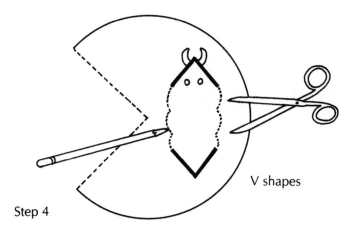

Step 4

V shapes

4. Draw two "V" shapes on the leftover plate piece as shown in the drawing. Then draw in lines to complete the bug. Cut out the bug shape.

5. Tape the bug body on top of the leg section.

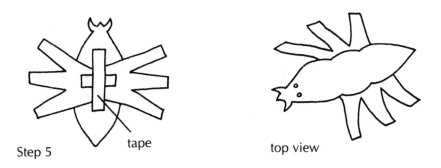

Step 5

tape

top view

Float It!   To make the bug skate faster, blow on it gently.

Experiment!   Make an entirely different sort of animal in the same way. If you cut off the middle legs and make a very long body, you can even make a crocodile!

TAD TURTLE

Tad is just about the size of a real baby turtle.

What You Need

1 styrofoam cup	scissors
1 styrofoam plate	pencil
	tape

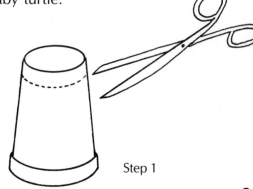

Step 1

What You Do

1. Cut around the cup near the bottom.

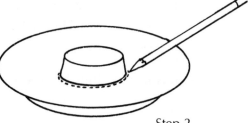

Step 2

2. Set the cut edge of the cup on the plate and draw around it.

3. Draw a turtle's head, feet, and tail on the circle.

4. Cut out the drawing and tape it over the open part of the cup.

Float It! Use a ballpoint pen to give Tad Turtle eyes and a grin.

Step 3

Experiment! Make bigger turtles by using styrofoam bowls or milkshake cups instead of small cups.

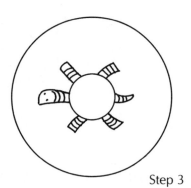

38

Step 4   tape

HOOP BALL

You can get styrofoam balls in many sizes at most craft stores. Ping-Pong balls work, too.

What You Need

Step 1

2 styrofoam plates   scissors
1 or more small   tape
  styrofoam balls

What You Do

match rims back to back

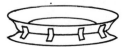

1. Cut the middles out of the two styrofoam plates.

Step 2

2. Match up the cut edges of the two plates, as in the drawing. *Don't nest them.*

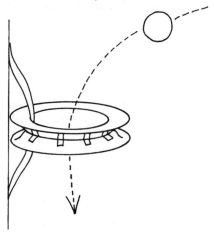

Play Ball! Tape the hoop to a dry tile or glass wall above the tub, or float the hoop in a pool or lake. You get 1 point each time the ball goes through (or into) the hoop. You get to keep the ball until you miss; then it's someone else's turn. Whoever gets to 20 points first, wins.

Experiment! Cut rims from styrofoam cups and float the rings for smaller targets that are harder to hit.

TROPICAL PENNY FISH

Turn your pool or tub into an aquarium by making lots of differently shaped fish for it. For ideas, get a book about tropical fish from your library.

What You Need

1 styrofoam plate	scissors
2 pennies	tape
1 small balloon	rubber cement
	pencil

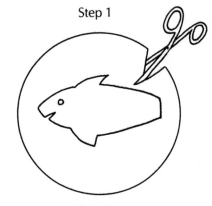

Step 1

What You Do

1. Draw any fish shape on the plate. Make it about the size of your hand, but leave off the tail.

2. Cut out the fish. Punch in an eye with the pencil. For pop eyes, poke a short piece of straw through the hole.

Step 2

3. Glue the pennies opposite one another at the lowest place on the fish. Tape over the pennies.

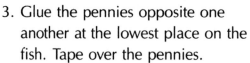

two sides of same fish

Step 3

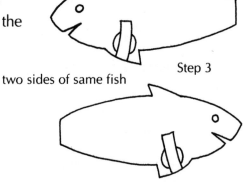

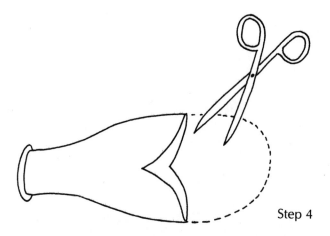

Step 4

4. Cut a tail shape from a balloon (you can use a broken one).
   Tape the tail to the fish.

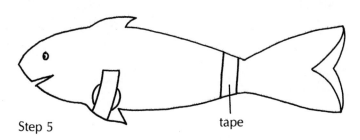

Step 5   tape

5. Tropical fish have wild and wonderful colors, so don't forget to
   decorate yours. See page 10 for lots of bright ideas.

Flick It!   Your Tropical Penny Fish will sink halfway into the
water. Flick its tail with your fingers to make it swim.

Experiment!   Cut out a bigger fish and use nickels instead of
pennies as weights. To make any size fish swim deeper in the
water, cut a bit off the top edge. Keep trimming the fish a little at
a time until it sinks far enough to suit you.

HYDRO-CRAFT

Not only does this spaceship fly—it also lands on water!

What You Need

6 styrofoam plates   scissors
                               tape

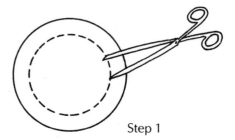

Step 1

What You Do

1. Set one plate aside. Cut the patterned rims off the other five plates. *Don't cut through the rims.*

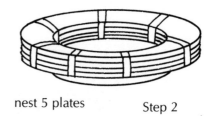

nest 5 plates   Step 2

2. Nest the rims together. Tape them into one thick hoop. Set the hoop on a table, cut part down.

3. Set the remaining whole plate upside down on the hoop. *Don't nest it in the hoop.* Tape the edges of the hoop and the plate together.

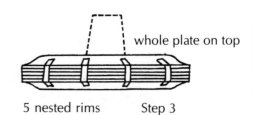

whole plate on top

5 nested rims   Step 3

Fly It! Hold your Hydro-Craft with the hole on the bottom. Then fling it with some wrist action, as you would throw a Frisbee. Let it land on the water.

Experiment! For an even spacier look, cut a hole a little bigger than the bottom of a styrofoam cup in the middle of your Hydro-Craft's deck. Push a cup, bottom up, through the hole.

SUN BOAT

You can make oars for this ingenious boat, or turn it into a sailboat!

What You Need

1 styrofoam plate

scissors
tape

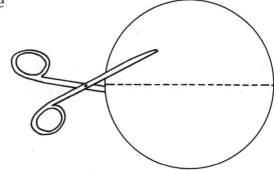

What You Do

1. Cut the plate in half.

Step 1

2. Nest the plate halves, so they look like one piece.

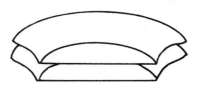

Step 2

3. Cut a strip about this wide ——————— (⅞ inch) off the straight edge. *Cut through both pieces at once.* Save the strips.

Step 3

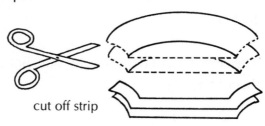

cut off strip

4. Match up the straight edges of the two pieces to make a boat shape. Hold them with crosswise pieces of tape.

5. Tape the boat lengthwise on *top and bottom*.

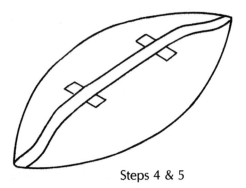

Steps 4 & 5

6. Tape a styrofoam strip across the boat near each end. Trim the ends of the strips to fit.

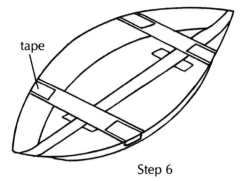

tape

Step 6

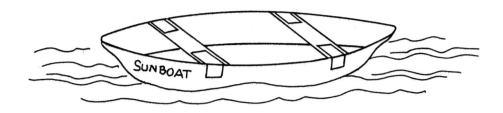

SunBoat

Float It!

Experiment! Make a smaller Sun Boat by cutting off a wider strip in Step 3.

ROW BOAT

Turn your Sun Boat into a Row Boat by making some easy oars.

What You Need

1 Sun Boat (page 43)   tape
2 straws   scissors
styrofoam scraps   pencil

What You Do

1. Make the Sun Boat on page 43.

2. Cut the bending ends off the straws and throw them away.

3. Cut two paddle shapes from styrofoam scraps. Tape a paddle shape to one end of each straw.

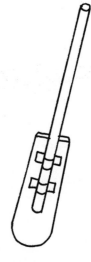

Step 3

4. Tape an oar to each side of the boat. Pinch the tape between the oar and the boat, so the oar can move.

Float It!

Experiment!   Cut out a styrofoam person to sit in the boat. Tape the person's hands to the oar ends. (Remember to tape the places like hips and knees that you want to bend, so they won't break.)

pinch tape here

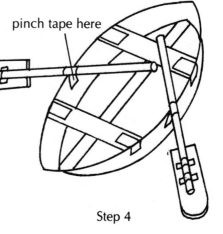

Step 4

SUPER SAILBOAT

This classy little sailboat is worth making—you can even set the sail! (Save all the styrofoam pieces because you will use almost every scrap!)

What You Need

1 Sun Boat (page 43)
1 styrofoam plate
1 penny
3 plastic straws

scissors
pencil
tape

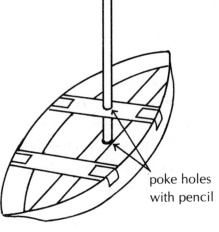

Step 2

slit

What You Do

1. *Make the Sun Boat (page 43).*

2. *Make the mast:* Cut two straws below the bend. Cut a slit in the end of one straw and slide it onto the other straw. Tape.

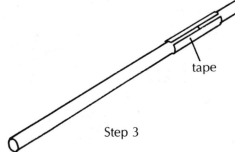

tape

Step 3

3. Poke a hole in the middle of one boat strip and in the boat bottom right below it.

poke holes
with pencil

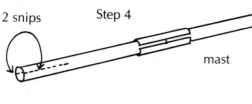

2 snips   Step 4

mast

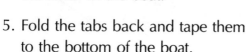

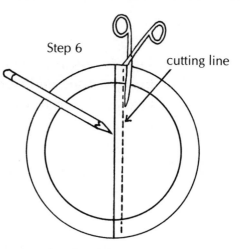

Step 5

snipped end of mast taped to bottom of boat

4. Make two snips this long —————— (about 1 inch) in one end of the mast. Poke the snipped end of the mast through the holes in the boat.

5. Fold the tabs back and tape them to the bottom of the boat.

Step 6

cutting line

6. *Make the sail:* Lightly draw a line across the middle of the plate. Cut across the plate about this far ——— (½ inch) from the line.

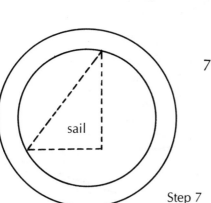

sail

Step 7

7. Draw a sail on the flat part of the biggest plate piece. Cut it out.

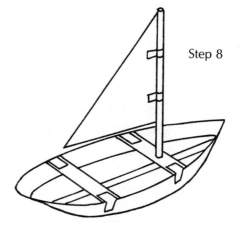

Step 8

8. Tape the sail to the mast.

9. *Make the keel:* Cut the other plate piece in half. Cut a triangle from one of the halves.

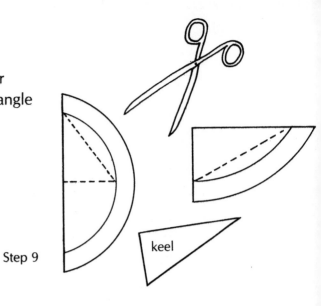

Step 9

keel

10. Tape the longest side of the triangle to the middle of the boat bottom. Tape the penny on it.

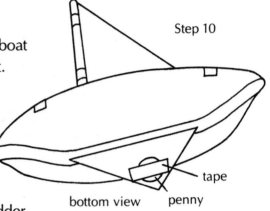

Step 10

bottom view   penny

tape

11. *Make the rudder:* Draw a rudder shape (see drawing) on the biggest scrap left.

rudder

Step 11

12. Cut out the rudder. Tape the longest edge to the bending end of a straw.

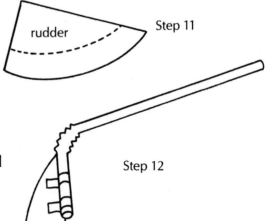

Step 12

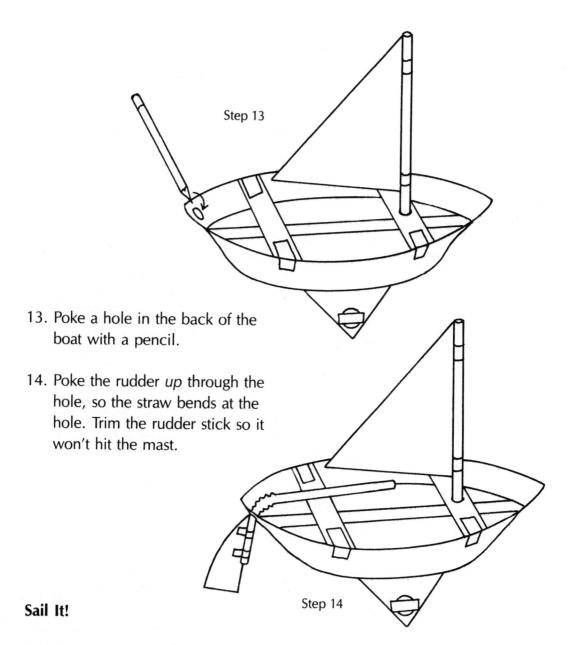

Step 13

Step 14

13. Poke a hole in the back of the boat with a pencil.

14. Poke the rudder *up* through the hole, so the straw bends at the hole. Trim the rudder stick so it won't hit the mast.

Sail It!

Experiment!   To set the sail, tape a short piece of thread to the free corner of the sail. Make some tiny snips on each side of the rudder. Pull the thread tight through one of the slits. You can change the position of the sail by using a different slit.

READY RIDER

Small, water-safe figures and dolls can go for a ride in this boat.

What You Need

2 styrofoam plates   scissors
2 styrofoam cups   pencil
                           tape

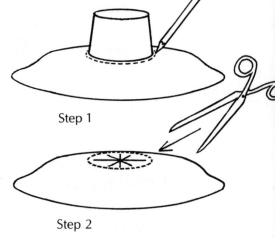

Step 1

What You Do

1. Cut a cup in half. Set the bottom half upsidedown on the middle of an upsidedown plate. Trace around it.

Step 2

2. Poke a hole in the middle of the circle. Make eight cuts from the hole to the circle. Push the tabs down.

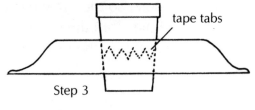

tape tabs

Step 3

3. Push a whole cup through the hole, bottom first. Tape the tabs to the cup.

4. Set the cup bottom in the middle of a right-side-up plate. Tape the plates together.

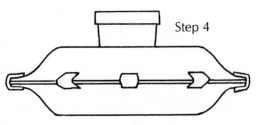

Step 4

Float It!   Carry cargo or small "passengers" in your Ready Rider.

Experiment!   Add a sail: Blow up a long balloon and tie it off. Use rubber cement to stick one end inside the cup.

POWER TOWER

Fill 'er up with water and away she goes!

What You Need

1 Ready Rider (page 50)
2 styrofoam cups
3 plastic straws

scissors
pencil
tape

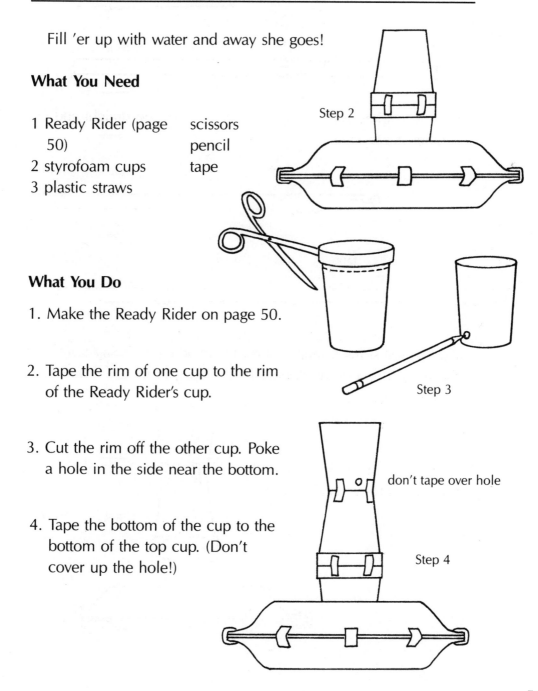

Step 2

Step 3

don't tape over hole

Step 4

What You Do

1. Make the Ready Rider on page 50.

2. Tape the rim of one cup to the rim of the Ready Rider's cup.

3. Cut the rim off the other cup. Poke a hole in the side near the bottom.

4. Tape the bottom of the cup to the bottom of the top cup. (Don't cover up the hole!)

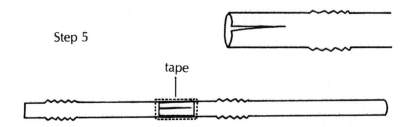

Step 5

tape

5. Slit the bending end of one straw. Slip it into the straight end of another straw. Tape.

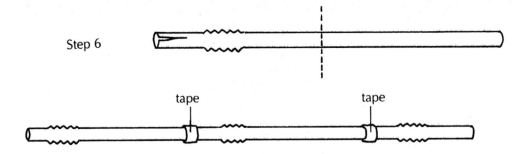

Step 6

tape   tape

6. Cut the last straw in half and slit the bending end. Slip it into the straight end of the double straw. Tape. (Now you have one l-o-n-g straw.)

7. Poke a hole near the edge of the boat. Go through both plates.

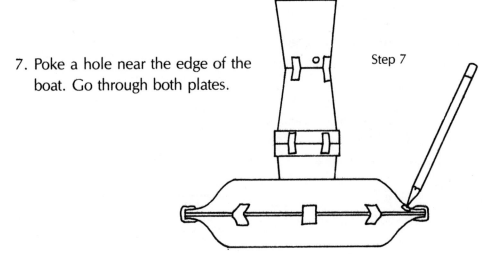

Step 7

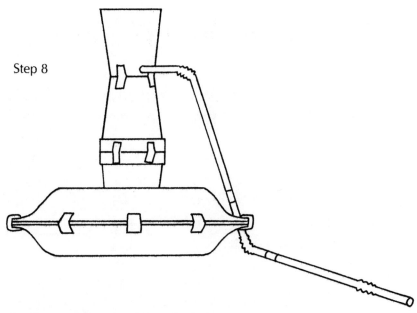

Step 8

8. Push the long straw up through the boat holes and into the hole in the top cup.

9. Tape the end of the straw inside the cup bottom. *Don't block the opening in the straw.*

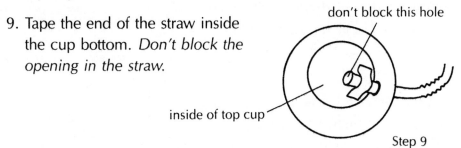

don't block this hole

inside of top cup

Step 9

Make your Power Tower Go!   Make sure the free end of the straw is under the water. For action, fill the top cup with water.

Experiment!   Make a *double* Power Tower boat! Instead of a single hole in the middle of the plate, make two holes next to each other. Set in two towers.

HORSESHOE PADDLER

Here's the prettiest little paddle boat you ever saw!
Don't let all the steps stop you—it's not hard at all.

What You Need

4 styrofoam plates	scissors
2 plastic straws	pencil
1 3-inch rubber band	tape
3 styrofoam cups	

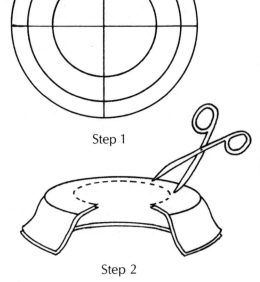

Step 1

What You Do

1. With a pencil, divide a plate into four equal parts. Draw a circle that's a little smaller than the bottom of the plate.

Step 2

2. Nest a second plate under the first. Cutting through both plates, cut out one pie-shaped piece. Then cut out the circle.

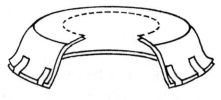

3. Nest the two pieces. Tape them into one horseshoe.

Step 3

4. Make *another* thick horseshoe (Steps 1-3). Tape the two horseshoes together rim to rim (see drawing). *Don't nest them.*

Step 4

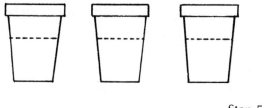

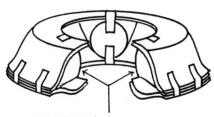

Step 5

cups, bottoms out

5. Cut the three cups in half around the middle. Squeeze the cups to fit, bottoms out, inside the horseshoe (see drawing). Tape. This helps make the boat strong.

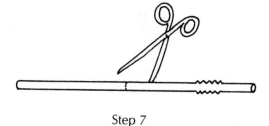

Step 6   bottom view

hole

poke hole on bottom of horseshoe shape

6. Poke a hole near each end of the horseshoe on the bottom, as shown.

7. Cut a straw in half. Poke the bending half through one of the holes.

Step 7

8. Loop the bent piece of straw through the rubber band. Then bend the straw into a circle, overlapping the ends. Tape the ends together.

Step 8

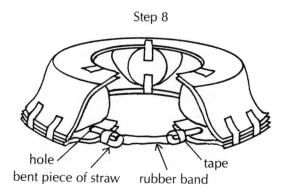

hole

bent piece of straw   rubber band   tape

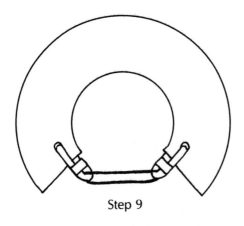

Step 9

9. Repeat Steps 7 and 8 for the second hole.

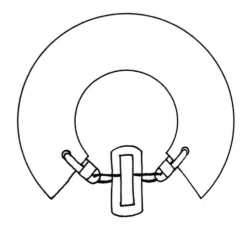

10. From a scrap of styrofoam, cut a rectangle for a paddle that will fit between the straws.

11. Slip the paddle through the rubber band. Tape both sides.

Step 11

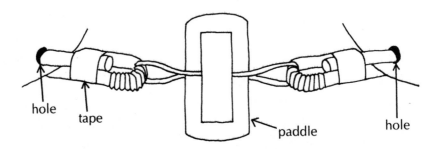

hole tape   paddle   hole

Make It Go! Wind up the paddle until the rubber band is tight. Set your Horseshoe Paddler in the water and let it go! (If it goes backwards, next time wind it the other way.)

Experiment! Cut a big duck head shape out of styrofoam. Make a slit in the front of your Horseshoe Paddler to fit the head into. (For laughs, make a horse's head instead!) Make wings to tape on the duck's sides by following Steps 1-3 for the Sun Boat (page 43).

EXPANDABLE STEAMBOAT

This ship is big to start with—but it can get bigger!

What You Need

3 styrofoam plates   tape
2 styrofoam cups   scissors
2 styrofoam burger   pencil
   cartons

What You Do

1. *Make the end pieces:* Nest the three plates together. Cut off about ⅓ from one side. *Cut through all the plates at once.*

2. *Make the middle piece:* Use one of the small pieces as a measure to cut the opposite ⅓ from *one* of the large pieces.

3. Tape the three large pieces together, as in the drawing.

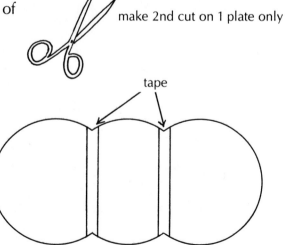

nest 3 plates

Step 1

Step 2

make 2nd cut on 1 plate only

tape

Step 3

4. *Make the smokestacks:* Mark a cup just under the rim. Make another mark on the opposite side of the cup, halfway up the side. Draw lines connecting the marks on both sides of the cup.

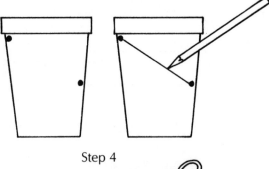

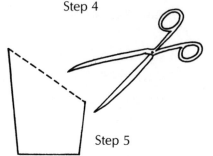

Step 4

5. Starting at the lowest point, cut along the line.

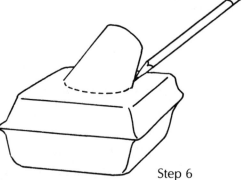

Step 5

6. Set the cut edge of the cup in the middle of a carton top. Trace around the cup.

7. Cut out the circle. Tape the cup to the hole from the inside of the carton. *Make the lowest side of the cup face the front of the carton.*

Step 6

8. Follow Steps 4-7 to make a second smokestack.

tape

cut hole

Step 7

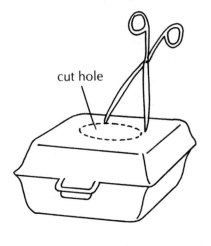

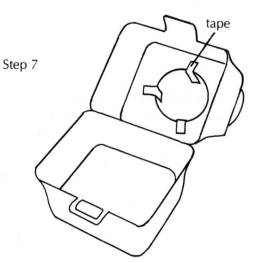

9. Cut portholes in the sides of each carton. Cut a bigger hole in each carton bottom.

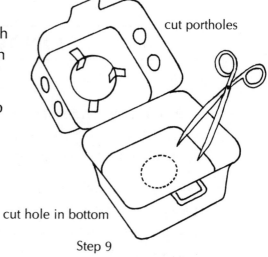

cut portholes

cut hole in bottom

Step 9

10. Set the cartons on the taped ship sections. Make sure the smokestacks point the same direction. Open the cartons and tape them in place across the holes in the bottoms.

11. Cut a triangle from one of the styrofoam scraps. Tape it to the front of the steamboat.

tape

triangle

Step 10

12. To make the Expandable Steamboat longer, simply add more middle pieces (Steps 1 and 2). Add as many smokestacks as you like (Steps 4-7).

Float It!   Open the "cabins" to stow passengers or cargo.

Experiment!   Make a Power Tower (pages 51-53) for the back smokestack. Fuel it with water.

Step 12

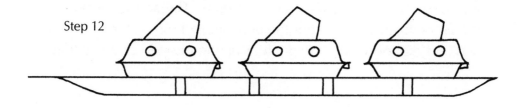

ON YOUR OWN

If you've gotten this far in the book, it must be time to start thinking up your own water toys. Being creative is just trying something a little bit different.

1. Give the directions a new twist. Look at the Experiment paragraph at the end of each set of directions. Each one suggests a way to give the toy on that page something extra. To make a different toy yourself, simply change a few of the steps, add something to the finished toy, or try making the toy bigger or smaller. Suddenly you'll be off in a whole new direction!

For instance, you can make the raft in the Experiment section on page 19 bigger by making longer straw pieces. Make them the way you did for the Power Tower on page 52. Then add more long balloons and make the straw pieces long enough to go across all the balloons.

2. Find new ways to play with things. Experiment with water-safe junk, your purchased water toys, or the toys you can make from this book. Here are some ideas to start with.

Make the Water Spinner on page 14, but use it as a squirter. Just pour water in through the straw, filling it up to the top. With your right hand, squeeze the end of the straw halfway shut. With your left hand, squeeze the water-filled balloon. Amazing!

Dip the plastic that holds a six-pack of soda cans in bubble soap and wave it through the air for an instant bubble-maker. Or create huge, gorgeous bubbles with just two plastic straws and a piece of string four times as long as a straw. Thread the string through both straws and knot the ends. Now hold a straw in each hand and dip the whole thing into a plastic dishpan or a roasting

pan full of bubble soap. Pull the strings taut and wave your bubble maker gently through the air. (Start with about ½ cup of shampoo or washing liquid like Ivory or Joy; add a little water at a time until the bubble soap works well.)

3. Experiment with new materials. Make sure the materials you use are soft, waterproof, and safe. Don't use anything that is hard, sharp, pointed, or breakable.

A piece of metalized Mylar, for example, makes a great unbreakable mirror. It will stick up on a slick wall with water, just like the Water Tiles on page 26. You can get Mylar at most art supply stores. Shiny and silvery, it has a mirrorlike look. If you peer into a piece of Mylar while you bend it, you will look really weird!

Make 3-D Water Tiles by gluing styrofoam balls or cut-out sponge shapes to Water Tiles (page 26) with rubber cement.

Cut inexpensive sponges into turtles, crocodiles, or other animals; glue them together with rubber cement. For an even simpler toy, cut sponges into blocks to stack into floating towers.

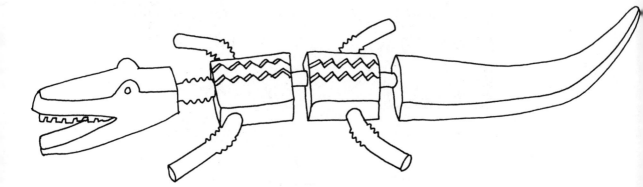

4. Put things together in new ways. Surely the authors of this book didn't think of *everything!* See what you can make with the materials listed on page 7, without repeating a toy that's already in the book!

5. Don't be afraid to make mistakes. There's nothing like a really awful mistake to set you off on a whole new way of thinking. Don't throw your mistake away. First, try to find ways to fix it. Your disaster might end up improving another toy, or leading to a wonderful new one!

6. Most of all, have fun with your water toys!

About the Authors

A former Peace Corps volunteer and teacher in high schools and colleges, MARY BLOCKSMA has written several children's books and textbook selections. Her accomplishments also include designing greeting cards and writing for magazines and newspapers. She lives in Healdsburg, California, where she works as a freelance writer. This book is her second collaboration with her brother Dewey; the first was the very popular *Easy-to-Make Spaceships That Really Fly,* also published by Prentice-Hall.

DEWEY BLOCKSMA is a physician who is now pursuing a career in art and design. His interest in toymaking began as a form of relaxation during his years working in hospital emergency rooms. The hobby eventually led to his designing easy-to-make water toys and spaceships! Mr. Blocksma lives in Okemos, Michigan.

About the Artist

ART SEIDEN, a member of the National Society of Illustrators, is well known for the clarity and verve of his illustrations. He has illustrated several books on various subjects for Prentice-Hall, including most recently *Computer Graphics Basics* by Lawrence Stevens. Mr. Seiden lives in Woodmere, New York.